AF243980

SHE SPEAKS

Ashley Joyce

To the ones who have always listened,

thank you.

CONTENTS

Introduction

I have always been the quiet girl observing in the corner. My parents said that I was so quiet as a baby that they joked I would be mute. Maybe I was as content to people watch then as I am today.

I started writing poetry as an outlet for my thoughts and emotions that felt a bit more artistic and self-expressive than a typical journal. I have often been afraid of voicing my opinions, emotions, beliefs, thoughts…anything, really. For whatever reason, I didn't believe they were important enough to share with anyone else. Or worse, people's perception of me would change for the worse. I'm learning that sometimes it's okay to say them aloud, regardless of how many people are listening. I didn't consider my writing worth pursuing until I started participating in the annual #escapril challenges by author Savannah Brown on Instagram and found that other people found something in my writing as well. I'm very good at considering my own work to be unassuming and underserved. It's a bad habit that I'm trying to break (slowly). However, with the amount of family and friends who continuously ask for a physical copy of my work, I figured it was about time I bit the bullet and appreciated the hard work I have put in over the years. This book is as much for me as it is for you as it is proof that I can write something worth publishing, something that is worth putting on a bookshelf.

This book contains a selection of poetry and prose from the past five or so years. It is a combination of #escapril poems as well as some new or reedited ones. I wanted to try and capture the range of emotions and changes I have experienced leaving my teenage years and entering into my twenties. Some of these are from a personal perspective, while others are taken from a fictional point of view. I hope you find your story threaded amongst these pages too.

the tree

out the back

that looked impossible to climb

its skin etched with age

an unknown number

its life held between

young and so very old

swinging like I was flying

touching the clouds with my nose

it was

mine

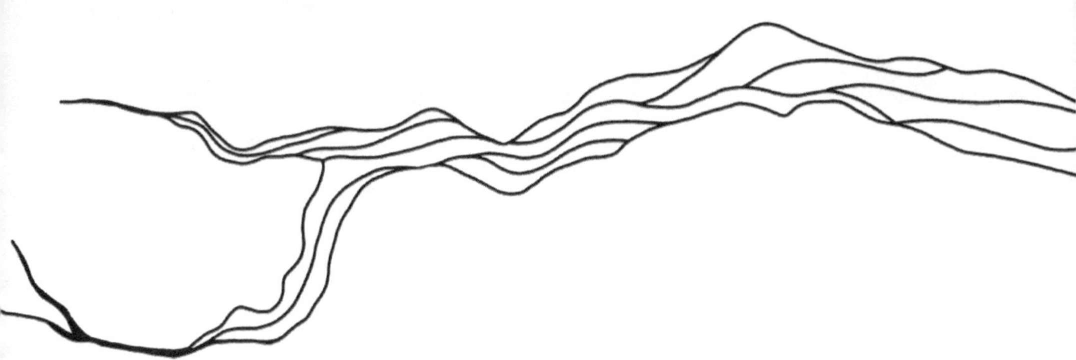

My window seat

7:00pm

       yellow

       yawns through

       my curtains

       a lingering

       hello and

       goodbye

7:40pm

       the clouds

       mix with

       the warmth

       of light

       like a melting pot

       of colour

8:00pm

       strokes of orange

       purple

       and pink

       dance through

       the blue

       oil in the sky

       with calculated steps

8:15pm

> i applaud the performance
>
> from my
>
> window seat
>
> as the
>
> stars begin to
>
> wake
>
> and the
>
> sun goes to sleep

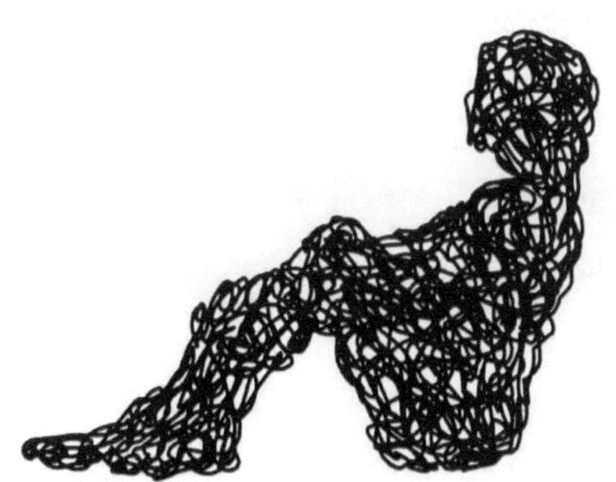

April showers

I hide in the corner

a drink in hand;

a drip,

drip,

dripping

from my tea bag.

Melted wax

forms an earthy scent;

a flick,

flick,

flickering of the flame.

April showers

knock at the window;

a tap,

tap,

tapping

on the glass,

as if to say hello,

autumn is here.

Nostalgia

I want to turn right instead of left

I want to take the winding road past the gumtrees and teddy bears

I want to chase the sunset in an unobscured sky

I want to cross the little bridge and pass the pine trees hiding life-sized dollhouses

I want to play an old CD that skips with every bump in the road

I want to watch the cows and sheep and horses living unhindered in their day

I want to pull into the driveway and be welcomed by an ever-growing garden

I want to open the painted red door and be welcomed by a familiar scent

But instead, I turn left and drive "home"

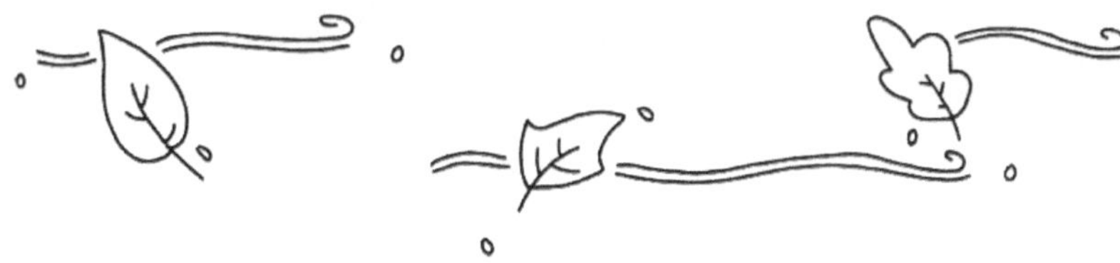

Thank you

No audience was full until you were in it

No wound was too deep that a kiss could not fix

Through sleepless nights, you sat with me

Through last minute projects you worked tirelessly

Every pain I felt, you felt, too

Every hug said I love you a thousand different ways

Tessellation

to the angels

on the clouds,

are our lives

a tessellation?

a polygon mesh

of repetitive events

a mix of

pentaprism faces

Just a crush

it's not like i notice the way the corners of his mouth twitch when
he is about to laugh,

or how his pupils grow at the mere mention of food.

i don't sit around and dream of the way his fingers flex when he
tries to comb back his hair in a moment of frustration.

if i was so distracted, would i notice this tree, and how the leaves
are looking brown?

or would i be thinking about the way his shoulders hunch when
the clouds begin to leak?

i don't walk into my room and smile at the sight of orange curtains
because they match his favourite socks.

his crooked nose is as forgetful as his tucked in graphic t-shirt that
still manages to fall lose from his creased, faded jeans.

if i really paid attention, i'd probably pick up silly things, like how
one eyebrow is arched slightly more than the other,

or maybe you are expecting me to mention his freckles on his
upper left cheek?

the simple fact i don't recall how his laugh echoes
through the floorboards should make it clear that i
don't think about him,

i don't think about him at all.

Kindred spirit

Being with you is forgettable, and I mean that in the best possible way

Time slips through my fingers absentmindedly

Like liquid gold

Your thoughts are stars, and I collect them in my pocket

But my pocket has a hole, so I can't recall a thing

I know I'm comfortable with you, but I can't explain how

You bring out my inner child and welcome her with open arms

You know me better than I know myself and that doesn't scare me

It's as if we have known each other through countless lives

Our bodies fit together like a puzzle designed by Fate

(She has a sense of humour, that's for sure)

For a pairing destined to be together

We are doomed to be far apart

Yet we are pulled together by an invisible string knotted around our pinkies

An unbreakable vow to always find each other again

And when we do meet up, the moment is gone too soon

The only recollection I have of you is left imprinted on my soul

Gardening

Friends are like flowers, like a rose bush in bloom. You plant a seed, and, over time, the earth creates room for the roots to expand and the stems to shoot straight. (Sometimes the best part about gardening is sitting in the wait.) One moment you have a bulb, protectively buried. The next, a bud, though seasons will vary. Until one day they blossom so bright that the sun makes them shine and you look at your friend, remembering lost time. Through every season and every storm, you must take care of your flowers. For, indeed, each one has special powers. There will, of course, be flowers that wither and grow frail, for only the strongest of seeds will prevail. Do not despair for the ones that do not make it to the new spring. There are plenty of flowers still to bloom if you are carefully watching. Sometimes the seeds need a little direction and sometimes we can be overprotective. Your flowers will thrive if you allow them the space to grow as they please and at their own pace. Every success will be your success, every stem that sprouts will nevertheless be able to fill your pockets with colourful pickings. So take heart, my dear gardener, for there are an abundance of seedlings.

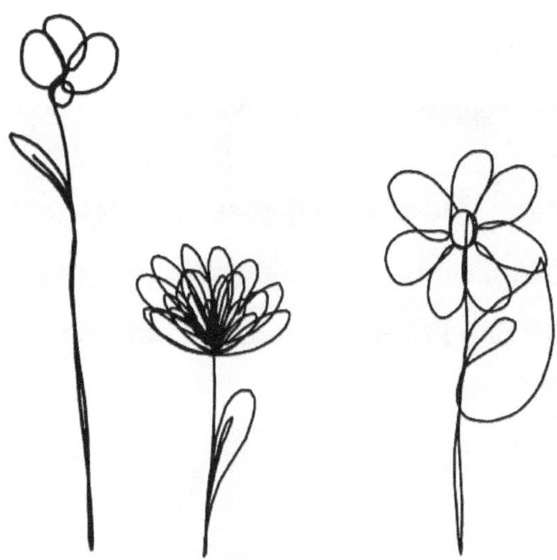

Synapse

We're lying on the bed and laughing about something I can't remember

The blanket pulled up to our necks as we huddle together

And all I can think of is

> *I want to be in this moment forever*

Where nothing really matters and yet you matter to me the most

We are so comfortable with each other   me in my own skin

We've established an unspoken understanding between the two of us through a single conversation

And I would never admit it out loud, but you bring me peace I have never known before

We talk about everything, and we talk about nothing, and we talk about your family and

You ask me what my plans are for Christmas, and I say I don't know we lie in silence

Looking up at the roof and I am desperate to hear your thoughts

> *What does the world look like through your eyes?*

I want to ask

But instead I make a comment on something I care nothing about

Part of me is worried that the moment is lost before I've had a chance to appreciate it

I try and find the magic again by redirecting the conversation, as hopeless a sentiment as that is

But you don't seem to notice, or you don't seem to care

And that makes me grateful

Superstition

If I don't text you back, will you cease to exist? Will your bones turn to dust and be swept away by the sea?

Will you be buried in an unmarked grave? Will I dance upon your broken flower bed?

Will I have to call your name three times to find you? Will you answer if I do?

Will you haunt me on my birthday? Will you be upset if I forget?

If I don't text you back, will your belongings be removed silently in the night? Will evidence of your existence be erased from the earth?

Will I drown myself in the unknowing guilt of it all?

Will you become a second shadow attached to my spine?

If I don't text you back, will you simply disappear? Will the hands of time keep pushing me forward while you're left behind?

Will the world keep turning without you in it?

Will I even notice you are gone?

If I don't text you back,

    will you cease to exist?

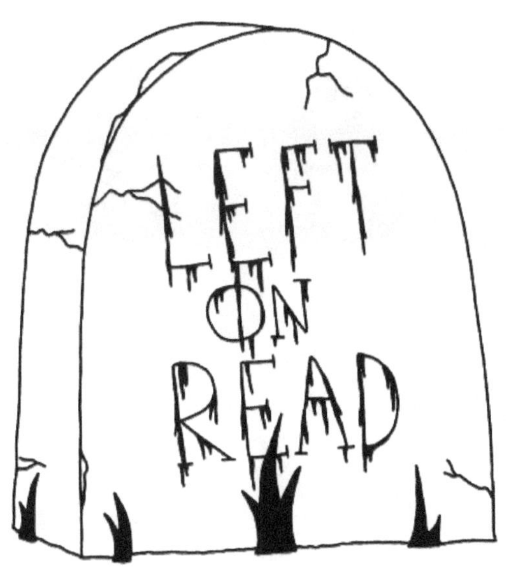

LEFT
ON
READ

Love like in the movies

Is it like the movies said?

Did it hurt when cupid struck your heart?

How did the butterflies escape your stomach?

Did someone come and tie your tongue?

Was there really a band playing music wherever you went?

Did you feel lighter than air when they called your name?

Was it hard to walk on weakened knees?

(I hope my palms don't become sweaty)

I bet you felt alive

And it only got better

When they revealed their love for you also

Tell me it's like the movies

Tell me it's just like they said

Idealistic

A couple walked past me laughing on the street and I wanted to be in that moment too

Regardless of whether the joke was funny or if I understood the context

I wanted their laugh to encapsulate me — to watch their relationship unfold with each breath

Maybe I'm naïve to think they were happy because they looked it at the time

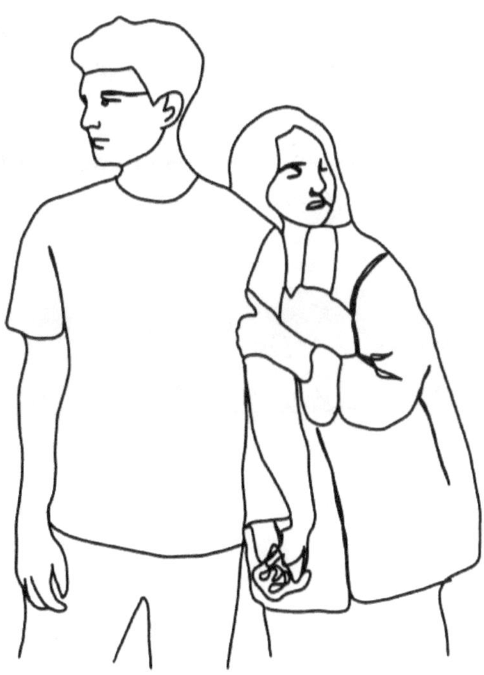

Blush

In the crook of the crescent moon you sleep, a glow upon my collarbone for comfort.

I wander the forests growing in your eyes but am not lost or alone. Leaf and moss on stone hold stories; whispered secrets of hopes, dreams, fears.

Like the setting of the sun, you hold a glow across the sky; golden hour with kisses of rose-hued blush upon my cheeks.

I am a painted daze held within the hands of a summertime artist who dreams of holding the brush morning, noon and night. Infectious and adventurous and resplendent.

Where upon the cliff you stand and welcome the sea salt evening air, deep shades of lavender and cornflower blue grow within the fields of waking stardust.

I am but scattered rock drawn as a constellation with you finding a connection between each of my points. You have given me my name.

Sensitive

It's hard being a helpless romantic

When you're afraid of walking away broken-hearted

Afraid of losing someone

Before it's even started

Limbs

Where do mine end and yours begin?

An intwined conversation

Held high at its finest hour

Our flesh and bone entangled

A combination of words mingled with sighs

Eyes wide, drinking in the picture

My lips on yours

Of course I taste first

The bite of your sweet nectar

The moment in passing

Lasting a lifetime (maybe longer)

Holding on to each other

A lover, surpassing all else

I am fine

I am a grenade held together by string and gum

A tipping point so thin it could be a hair upon Fate's head

A thousand passing instances of misplaced words

'I'm sorry' used too frequently as a superfluous excuse

But don't worry, my attention is in your palm

Can you not see my eyes reading the script upon your lips?

Intentionally trying to make you feel heard

Do not peer too closely, the mask stitched into my skin

Will crumble at the slightest touch, please handle with care

Look upon this porcelain face and ask how I am

I will say I am fine I am fine I am fine I am fine I am fine

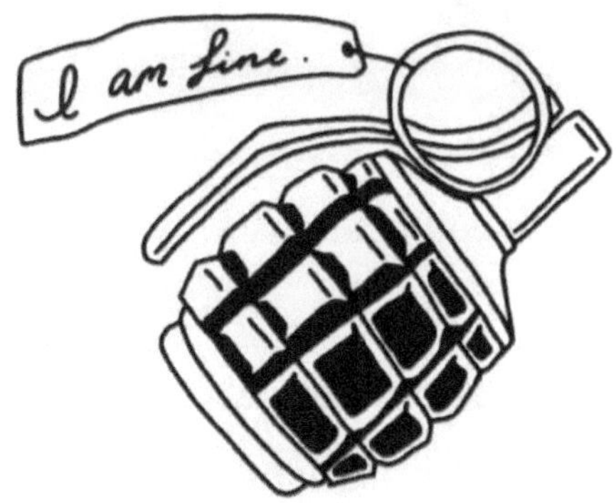

Attention

the eyes the eyes the eyes

the mouth the lips the smiles

the fingers tapping on the table

forgotten forgiven judged

never remembered beyond the moment

crazy spiralling mind-numbing cries

it all must lie behind

the eyes the eyes the eyes

watching movement from behind

their easy remarks and polite replies

regressed repressed redundant

my thoughts are not important

never let the girl be heard

i am but a doll to observe

the eyes the eyes the eyes

a storybook bound with clever white lies

a nod to keep them engaged

my neck bouncing until it breaks

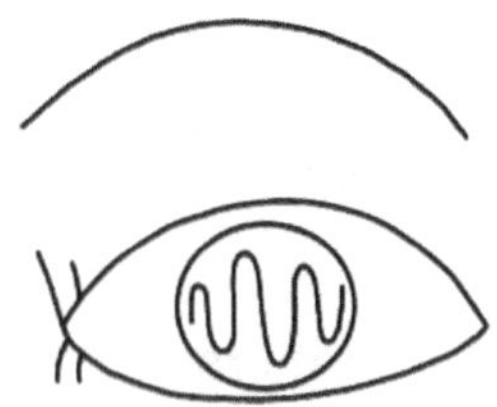 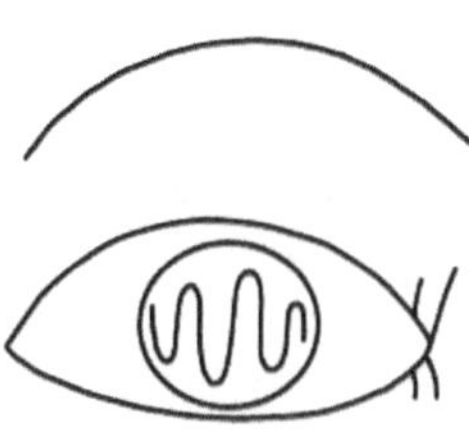

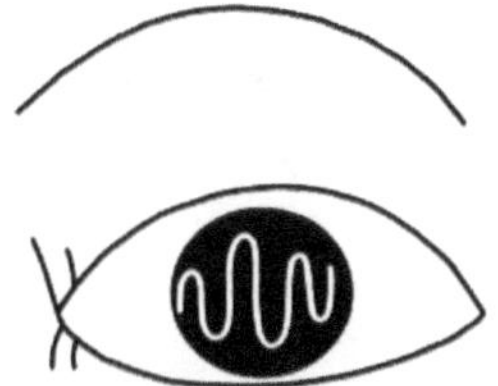 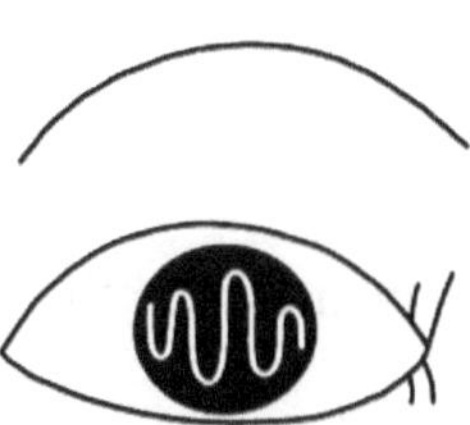

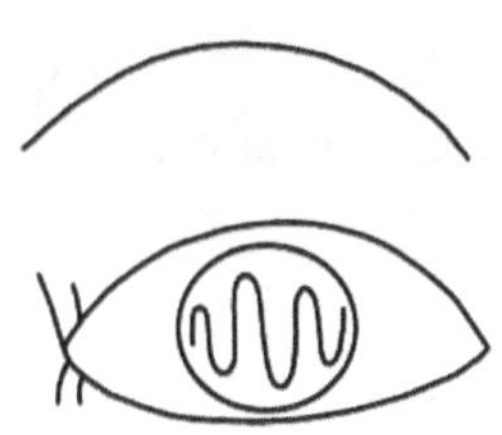 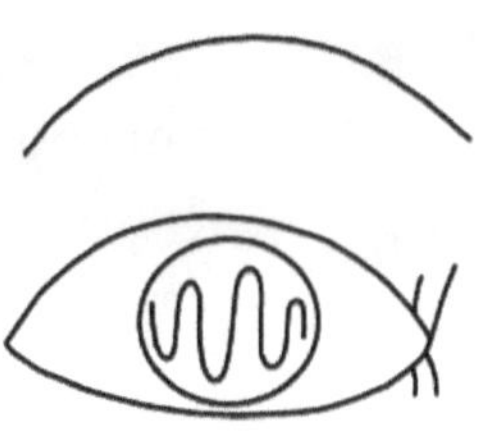

Fear

Like shifting powder down the barrel of a gun loaded by a madman,

I am the dust left upon every surface and the grime coated under
your nails.

Bottled up thoughts pressing against glass until it cracks, splits —

    Listen!

You feel me in your pulse as it quickens.

Let me in; I will be your friend.

Trust me like you trust the break of thunder and I will not lead you
astray.

Your guide amongst the horrors of living.

    Listen...

Patiently lying in wait in the fractures of your mind; carnivorous
termites,

Counting the shadows that claw along your floor, your walls, your
windows.

You may not need me now, but you will need me soon.

    Listen.

Cardboard box pedestal

Building a pedestal for me only left me with one option — to fall

All you'd heard of me were lies twisted into legends

I was trained to put on a show, and you fell for the sleight of hand

You didn't want to believe that on the inside I was as broken as you

I was meant to be your guiding light, but the ocean pulled us under

If you were the Titanic, I was the ice all around you

I had gotten so good at playing pretend that you saw it as my reality

Now I am nothing but the broken image of who you wanted me to be, but could never become

I'm sorry

There is so much being said in the silence between us; a thunderous rumble caught in a storm of our own making. My image of you is distorted and twisted. You've become a stranger sitting across from me.

We've built a towering wall with the silence between us; to wade through the murky middle air would be a suicide mission. Is it worth the risk?

We're both too afraid to break the silence between us and we're both unsure what to do next. I am scared my mouth is filled with poisoned darts that will pierce you through the veil.

I am drowning in the silence between us, but you are oblivious to my cries. Disoriented by the waves of shame and anger and confusion and sadness leaves no surface to break for air.

What more needs to be said in the silence between us;

Sweater weather

Here we are together

Me, wearing your sweater

The warmth of your body
and the flames of the fire

Mingle together into a
curling spire

Drink after drink

While wearing your
sweater

I remember when you said
you'd be my forever

But liars are good at
having hearts of stone

You always made me feel
hopelessly alone

In your sweater

Forgetting what mistakes
mattered

Ignoring all the telltale
signs of a reoccurring
pattern

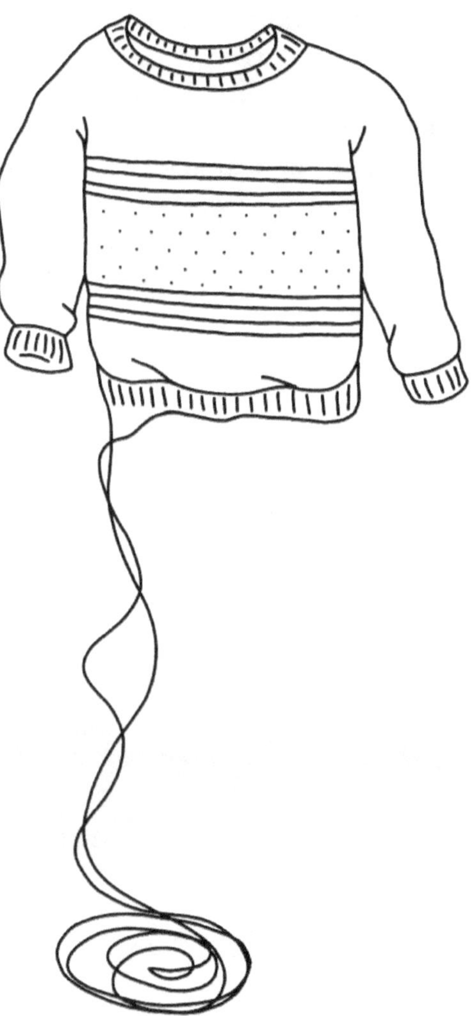

For a moment

i rolled over and felt your body, a calming rhythm of normality. i brushed the hair away from your eyes; no need for light to find each freckle upon your cheeks. from the head i traced down your back to the shirt worn beyond repair. i stroked your fingers and curled my nails around your knuckles until each joint was against mine. my eyes closed as my lungs synced with yours; the drowsiness of the night air finally finding me. when i opened my eyes, there was nothing but the sheets that used to smell like you.

White lies

We sat; you spoke.

I replied (I tried).

Simple topics that led nowhere in particular — work, home, life.

I watched as your mind raced through idea after idea, grasping at strings that would lengthen our conversation.

My mind was matching pace, but we were on opposite sides of the brain.

I said, 'Yes,' and, 'No,' and, 'We absolutely need to plan to do that.'

When really my mind was screaming, 'How do I tell them?' and, 'Will they be okay without me?'

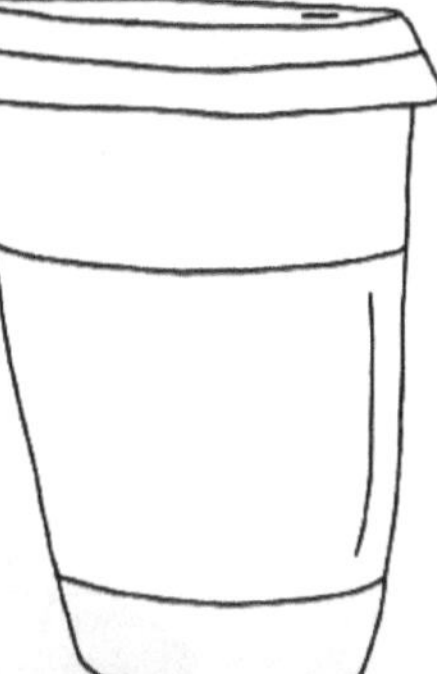

My coffee was cold, but I drank it to be occupied; your mouth kept moving, but no sound was coming out.

Baggage

if you tipped me over and hung me by my feet, would my insides tumble out like a monotonous monologue no one wants to hear? my deepest secrets shaken lose to clatter to the floor in an embarrassing display of vulnerability. i might rattle like a baby's toy with each step that i take. if you tipped me over and hung me by my feet, i might release every feeling i've ever had at once; you don't want to see the mess that could be. you would feel obliged to clean it up, but i don't want your pity. your eyes would hold an apology that isn't yours to give. if you tipped me over and hung me by my feet, you might loathe what you see. you will hold the same contempt as i do for myself. i want you to understand me, but only the parts i choose to display. if you tipped me over and hung me by my feet, you might see too much.

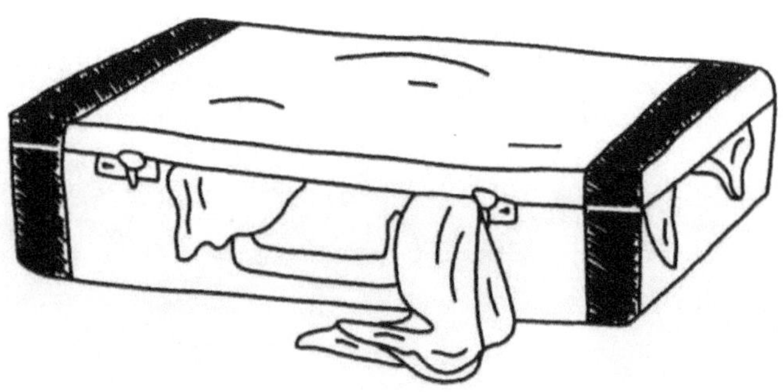

Trying to be good

How are you?

> *my week has been a trainwreck. i've ignored every message on my phone. i'm sick of eating the same thing every day. i don't have the energy to go grocery shopping. i need to see my friends. i don't want to leave my bed. i have the desire to travel but it's getting harder every day. my head is too loud. i need a shower. i have a creative itch that needs to be scratched. i have a crippling fear of failure. i don't want to go to work. the cost of living has gone up again. i'm so lazy. i love being alone. i crave human connection. people keep dying. i don't want to study. i'm worried i'm not smart enough. i have so many privileges. i think i might be crazy. i'm so ungrateful. i'm worried i missed my moment. life feels too short. everything is moving too fast. help me help me please help me help me help.*

I'm good.

Dissociation

The fingers fumble with the keys until they fit into

the ignition. The engine hums lazily as the head turns to

pull out of the carpark.

The hands turn the wheel to line the boxed car

with the tarmac stripes.

The eyes wander from

the road to

the other vehicles to

the clouds in the sky and back to the road.

The left hand moves to increase the volume of

the radio. The head turns into oncoming traffic.

The foot places pressure on the accelerator. The

right hand signals to merge. The eyes wander from

the road to

the traffic lights to

the grass dancing in the breeze and back to the road.

The foot brings the car to a stop. The left hand engages the

handbrake. The fingers turn the key, and the feet

carry the body inside.

Strange behaviour

Sometimes I can get lost in a world behind my eyes

Instead of listening to the people sitting by my side

Who talk about the weather, and who talk about their day

Pulling me into a waking dream where their voices fade away

I wander through my mind, which is a vast and open land

A place of stories, songs and heroes who fall hand in hand

With adventures of love and loss; kings and queens so great

A thousand stories told in one, a thousand more stories to create

For in those places in my mind, the story is entwined

In mystery and magic and systems so combined by

My love for art and my love for words and for happily ever afters

That I do not want these stories to end, I am my own director, writer, crafter

I've tried to explain the visions, of the worlds that I can see

But I'm often met with looks of disdain or mild curiosity

It makes me wonder, do people not have a story pulling at their heart?

Do people not know what it's like to feel whole, unbroken and torn apart?

It is a hazard, I know, to have a mind such as this,

Where I accidentally find myself trying not to miss

The words that leave the lips of another in front of me

But it's difficult when I so desperately want to escape reality

So when you speak and my eyes gloss over and I look into the distance

And when I do not reply or hardly utter a sentence

Just know that I am listening, I am really trying my best

But the ways in which I speak sound a lot better in my head

The daydreamer

a projector room behind the eyes alights within her mind / a world spun by a dreamer who is not yet ready for slumber / caught in a web of her own making / seconds pass with the silent tick of a clock / a play caught at intermission / a thousand and one moments to decide upon / narrative threads ready to be woven / cast and crew and director are one / everything must be / perfect / the dreamer cannot sleep until the final act is through / like puppets on a string / conducted to perform again and again / it is all an act / a vicarious waltz upon a glittering tightrope / with sword to chest the curtains fall / hollow silence awaits the end / an unravelled thread that will never be cut lose

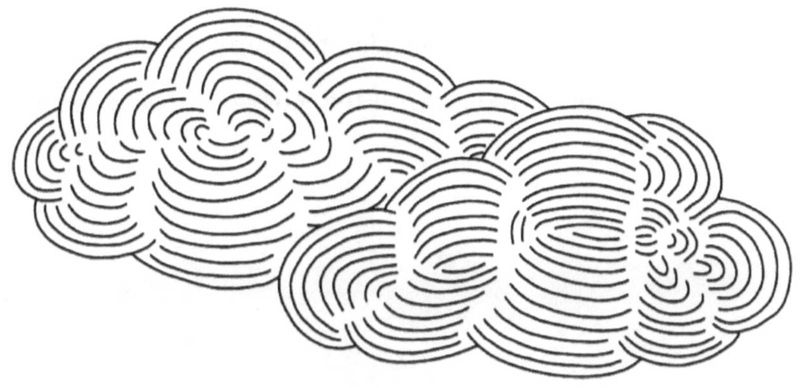

Magic hour

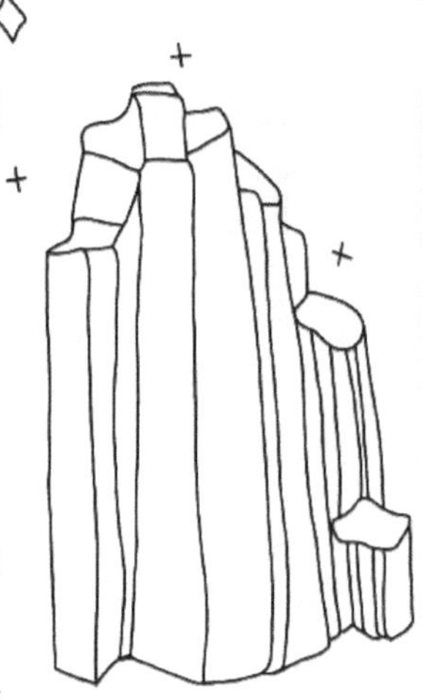

The asphalt sparkles in the afternoon sun and I can't help thinking,

Is this it?

Is this where the magic goes to die?

Rolled into our manmade earth to be walked upon as concrete jungles.

No one cares where it came from; its ashes coat our lungs.

Too busy focussing on the next best thing. Oblivious to the details in life's splendour.

We've forgotten about the magic; left to sleepwalk through our day.

Pulling our feet along the ground like we're connected to apathy's ball and chain.

Me

sometimes i walk to the park for no other reason than to smell the flowers

sometimes i step onto a train with no destination because i want to find it along the way

if you see me tapping my fingers, i'm playing along to a song you can't hear   join in if you like

but the celebratory dances in my room are for me and me alone

i've been called a daydreamer but i think that's an oversimplification

for i dare to dream at all hours of the day and night and the seconds lost between

the cracks within my skin that hold every part of who i am

precious moments held in the palm of my hand   crushed in my pocket

Lost things

i read people like a book without pages

piecing together an unwoven tale about an unsung hero

an invitation lying in wait

ask ask ask

and i'll tell you

a whispered song sung by lost souls

forgiven, forgotten, forsaken

a heart stitched to a tattered sleeve

i am a witness to confessionals upon a creased face

who were you?

who did you want to be

how many dragons have you slain?

how many demons sleep in your shadow?

i encapsulate you in a linear painting of string

not the artist but the curator

granted access to hidden tomes

scrolls left to hold dust upon a darkened shelf

unfolded in an unceremonious mess

i don't accept apologies from the lips of the storyteller

delicately told by one who feels undeserving

unloved

i see it all

accepted and bound

logged away with the other lost things

37

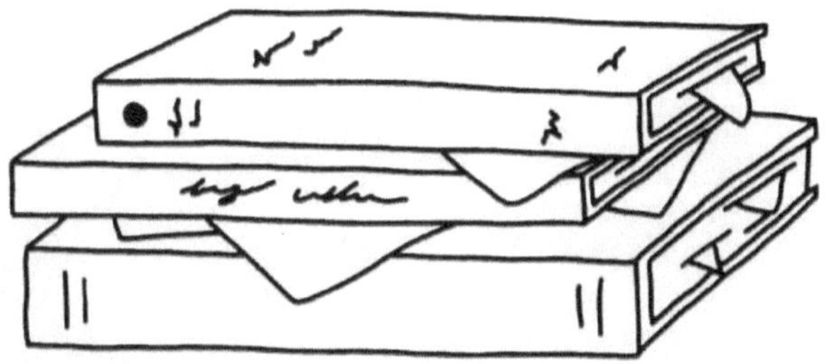

Time

One thing they never tell you about growing up is how much you're going to lose. It's a race with Father Time. His shadow is always there, running beside you. It's a race you unknowingly entered, a medal you don't want. An impossible challenge; unwinnable. Days turn to months; months turn into years. You're not living, you're trying to survive. Father Time cheated before you even began. His claws sink into your back before you understand; you've lost.

Safe space

The thing I like about the city at night

Is the stillness in the streetlights

Driving down a watered road

Taking the longest way back home

Listening to the leaves blow in the breeze

Makes my soul feel at ease

It's quiet, it's peaceful

It's like watching the earth fall asleep

There's something about the starlit sky

That tells me everything will be alright

Left behind

When the party's over
and there's nothing left to say,
people trickle out the door
and slowly fade away.

When the party's over
and the music has died down,
there are traces of what happened,
echoes that dance around.

When the party's over,
someone has to stay behind
to clean up the mess that
others have left for them to find.

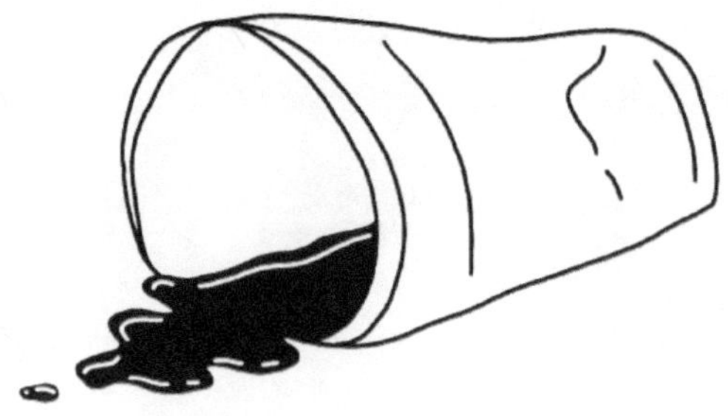

This is goodbye

Lament with me awhile as the wind whistles our woes

Misery mixed up in mystery of long forgotten vows

If only we could open the door to our old abode

Now bricked up and overgrown with brambles and roses

Yesterday I found yet another postcard of your yearning

Long departed desperations written in wet ink

Ramblings on the rain and why rivers rapidly dry out

You are the overgrown gardenias guarded by my guilt

My heart holds on too tightly to the hollow hopes in my hand

Twilight

Soon the stars will slink into view and rest

Upon the silver tongue's back

Shadows will dance between flickering flames

And laughter will echo down the street

But then, silence

Settling on your doorstep with a

Goodnight kiss

Caressing the air into stillness

Until all is where it should be

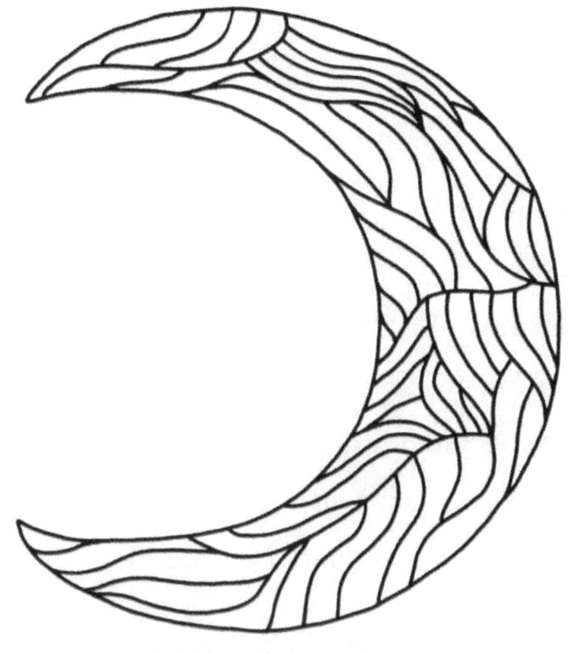

Goodnight

I have a daydreamer's soul

That is surrounded by a thirst for knowledge

A hunger for more

Always more

Each night I push the daydreamer into a fantasy

Safely tucked into bed

By the ghostly hands of

Yesterday's fear

'Dream, my sweet, dream.

Sleep in the peace of tomorrow,

Knowing no one can harm you.

Fly through the clouds and reach for the stars.

This battle is not your fight.'

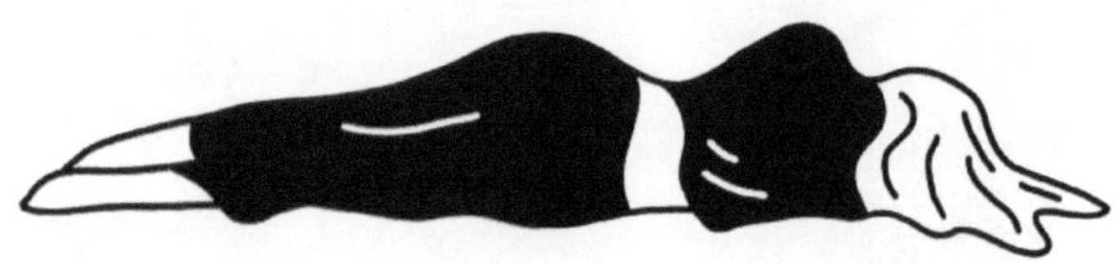

Acknowledgements

This book would have never seen the light of day without the encouragement, creativity and constant pestering from a selection of people.

To my parents, Cris and Cath, for never doubting my abilities and for pushing me to pursue my creative endeavours. You surrounded me with literature from a young age and for that, I thank you.

To my brothers, Nathaniel and Toby, for being constantly subjected to my work, whether or not they asked for it, but being proud of it, nonetheless.

To my grandad, Bruce, and Joan, for showing me how powerful the written word can be, even if it feels like only a handful of people will ever read it. I am in awe of all you have accomplished over the years.

To Helga, Bryan, Vanessa, Lincoln and Imogen, thank you for your consistent stream of inspiration from a variety of literature and authors. You have always made me feel like my work was a welcome addition in our family of writers.

To my other extended family members, watching you pursue your dreams regardless of setbacks has always inspired me to pursue mine. I cheer on the sideline for every little win you have.

To my group of friends, Betul, Meral, Bethany, Elly, Aseel and Ayah, you are the driving force behind almost anything I accomplish. You fuel the fire in my soul and inspire my creative spirit. You are each a kindred spirit and I love you all deeply.

Lastly, a big thank you to my mum and Ayah, for editing this work for me. You don't know how much I appreciate you setting time aside for a silly little project such as this.

About the Author

Ashley grew up in the capital of Australia. Being surrounded by all forms of literature from a young age welcomed her into the world of storytelling. She is now studying her Master's in Melbourne where she spends most of her time reading, writing, painting and daydreaming (sometimes all at once).

She is also terrible at social media, but if you want somewhere to find her, you can follow her Instagram: @herforgetmenots

...

For more information on #escapril visit:

@letsescapril

@savbrown